IMAGES OF
SCOTLAND

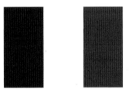

SCHOTTLAND   ESCOCIA   L'ÉCOSSE

LOMOND

This edition published in 2012 for Lomond Books Ltd
Broxburn, EH52 5NF, Scotland
www.lomondbooks.com

Karen Fitzpatrick has worked in book publishing for many years, some of which she spent in London. She now lives in her native Scotland with her family and works as an editor and writer. Her particular areas of interest include Scottish culture and literature.

Front cover: Castle Sinclair Girnigoe, Caithness
Back cover: Eilean Donan Castle, Loch Duich, Dornie (page 29)

All images are copyright © V.K. Guy Ltd except the following:
p48 © 2006 TopFoto/J. Smith; p75 © 2005 TopFoto/Barnes;
p81 © 2005 TopFoto/Matt Miller; p92 Shutterstock/© Bill McKelvie

Thanks to: Mike and Carl at V.K. Guy, Vanessa Green, Chelsea Edwards, Chris Herbert, Julie Pallot, Mike Spender, Frances Bodiam and Nick Wells.

For this multi-language edition, many thanks to Julia Rolf, Susan *et al.* at WordSmiths Translators Ltd., Bettina Dietrich *et al.* at Print Company, Jordi Nolla and Christine Delaborde.

Created by and copyright © 2012 Flame Tree Publishing Ltd
www.flametreepublishing.com

14 16 15
5 7 9 10 8 6 4

ISBN 978 1 84204 216 8

A copy of the CIP data for this book is available from the British Library.

Printed in China

IMAGES OF
SCOTLAND

  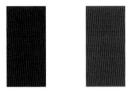

SCHOTTLAND   ESCOCIA   L'ÉCOSSE

KAREN FITZPATRICK

LOMOND

CONTENTS

INHALT · ÍNDICE · SOMMAIRE

THE HEBRIDES, ORKNEY AND SHETLAND ISLES

The islands off the northern coast of Scotland have a unique beauty, with their magical stone circles, wild landscapes, impressive castles, ruined abbeys and thriving fishing villages.

Die vor der schottischen Nordküste liegenden Inseln mit ihren magischen Steinkreisen, wilden Landschaften, beeindruckenden Burgen, Klosterruinen und blühenden Fischerdörfern sind von einzigartiger Schönheit.

Auf Seite 127 finden Sie ein Glossar mit schottischen Begriffen.

Las islas de la costa norte de Escocia tienen una belleza única, con sus círculos de piedra mágicos, paisajes salvajes, impresionantes castillos, abadías en ruinas y prósperos pueblos de pescadores.

Tiene a su disposición un glosario con términos específicos escoceses en la página 127 de esta guía.

Les îles au large de la côte nord de l'Écosse sont d'une beauté sans pareil avec leurs cercles de pierres magiques, paysages sauvages, châteaux spectaculaires, abbayes en ruine et villages de pêcheurs florissants.

Vous trouverez un glossaire de mots spécifiquement écossais en page 127 de ce livre.

Standing Stones of Callanish

LEWIS

This complex arrangement of 50 stones forms the shape of a Celtic cross and was erected between 3,000 and 4,000 years ago.

Diese komplexe Formation von 50 Steinen der Megalithkultur erinnert an ein keltisches Kreuz. Sie wurde vor 3000 bis 4000 Jahren errichtet.

Este complejo monumental de 50 piedras toma la forma de una cruz celta y fue erigido hace entre 3.000 y 4.000 años.

Cet ensemble complexe de 50 pierres, en forme de croix celtique, fut érigé il y a environ 3000 à 4000 ans.

Tolsta Head

LEWIS

The Isle of Lewis's most breathtaking beaches can be found on the east coast and are massively populated with a diverse wildlife.

Die atemberaubendsten Strände der Insel Lewis liegen an der Ostküste und haben eine mannigfaltige Fauna und Flora.

Las playas más importantes de la isla de Lewis se encuentran en la costa este y están densamente pobladas por una fauna diversa.

Les plages les plus impressionantes de l'île Lewis se trouvent sur la côte Est et sont fortement peuplées par une faune variée.

Seilebost

HARRIS

The Norse meaning for Harris is 'high land' and this beautiful area boasts mountains, sea lochs, coastal islands and white sandy beaches.

Die altnordische Bedeutung von Harris ist „Hochland". Diese wunderschöne Gegend bietet Berge, Meeresbuchten, der Küste vorgelagerte Inseln und weiße Sandstrände.

Harris significa 'tierra alta' en escandinavo, y esta bella zona cuenta con montañas, *sea lochs*, islas costeras, y playas de arena blanca.

Harris signifie "high land" ("hautes terres") en norrois. Cette belle région possède des montagnes, des lacs salés, des îles côtières et des plages de sable blanc.

Portree

SKYE

Skye's main town, Portree's name derives from the Gaelic for 'King's Port', referring to King James V's (1513–42) arrival in 1540.

Der Name von Skyes größter Stadt, Portree, ist vom Gälischen für „Hafen des Königs" abgeleitet und bezieht sich auf die Ankunft von König James V. (1513–1542) im Jahr 1540.

Pueblo principal de Skye, Portree significa Puerto del Rey en gaélico, refiriéndose a la llegada del Rey Jaime V (1513–42) en el año 1540.

Le nom "Portree", ville principale de Skye, provient de 'King's Port' en Gaélique ('Port du Roi'), en référence à l'arrivée du Roi Jacques V (1513-42) en 1540.

Neist Point

SKYE

The most westerly point on the Isle of Skye, Neist Point offers superb vistas and has a spectacular lighthouse dating from 1909.

Der westlichste Punkt der Insel Skye, Neist Point, bietet mit seinem eindrucksvollen Leuchtturm aus dem Jahr 1909 eine herrliche Aussicht.

El punto más occidental de la Isla de Skye, Neist Point, ofrece unas vistas espléndidas y cuenta con un espectacular faro del año 1909.

Le point le plus à l'ouest de l'île de Skye, Neist Point avec son phare spectaculaire de 1909, offre un superbe panorama.

The Cuillin

FROM SLIGACHAN, SKYE

The spiked peaks of the Black Cuillin hills, which are composed of basalt and gabro, can be seen from many vantage points.

Die spitzen, aus Basalt und Gabbro bestehenden Gipfel der Bergkette Black Cuillin können von vielen Aussichtspunkten aus betrachtet werden.

Los picos afilados de las colinas Black Cuillin, que están compuestas de basalto y gabro, se pueden ver desde muchos miradores.

Black Cuillin, ce massif montagneux aux cimes hérissées composées de basalte et d'euphotide (gabbro), peut être admiré depuis de nombreux points d'observation.

Castle Moil

KYLEAKIN, SKYE

Castle Moil dates back to the tenth century. Now in ruins, the castle once served as a lookout post and fortress.

Castle Moil stammt aus dem 10. Jahrhundert. Das jetzt in Ruinen liegende Schloss diente einst als Beobachtungsposten und Festung.

El Castillo Moil, siglo X, se encuentra en la actualidad en ruinas. En el pasado sirvió de atalaya y fortaleza.

Le Château Moil remonte au Xème siècle. Maintenant en ruines, il servait jadis de poste de guet et de forteresse.

Torosay Castle

MULL

Built in 1858 in the Scottish baronial style by architect David Bryce (1803–76), part of Torosay Castle is still used as a family home.

Im Jahr 1858 vom Architekten David Bryce (1803–1876) im Scottish Baronial Style erbaut, wird ein Teil des Torosay Castle immer noch als Familiensitz genutzt.

Construido en el año 1858 en estilo señorial escocés por el arquitecto David Bryce (1803–76), una parte del Castillo Torosay aun se utiliza como residencia familiar.

Construit en 1858 dans le style seigneurial écossais par l'architecte David Bryce (1803–76), une partie du château de Torosay est toujours utilisée comme maison familiale.

Tobermory

MULL

Tobermory, Mull's capital, is characterised by its main street and the quirky, brightly painted houses that wrap around the peaceful bay.

Tobermory, die Hauptstadt der Insel Mull, ist von ihrer Hauptstraße und den pittoresken, bunt bemalten Häuser geprägt, die sich ans Ufer der ruhigen Bucht schmiegen.

Tobermory, capital de Mull, se caracteriza por su calle principal y por las extravagantes casas pintadas de colores vivos que envuelven esta bahía tranquila.

Tobermory, la capitale de Mull, est caractérisée par sa rue principale et ses maisons originales peintes de couleurs vives qui longent cette baie paisible.

Iona Abbey
IONA

Iona Abbey was founded by St Columba and his Irish followers in AD 563, and attracts around 140,000 worshippers every year.

Iona Abbey wurde von Columban von Ionia und seinen irischen Anhängern 563 n. Chr. gegründet und zieht jährlich rund 140 000 Gläubige an.

La Abadía Iona fue fundada por S. Columba y sus seguidores Irlandeses en el año 563. Atrae a alrededor de 140.000 fieles cada año.

L'abbaye d'Iona a été fondée par Saint Colomba et ses disciples irlandais en 563 apr. J.-C. et attire environ 140,000 fidèles par an.

Kiloran Bay
COLONSAY

Kiloran Bay, an inlet on the north-west coastline of the tiny island of Colonsay, is one of the most beautiful beaches in Scotland.

Kiloran Bay, eine Bucht an der Nordwestküste der winzigen Insel Colonsay, hat einen der schönsten Strände in Schottland.

Kiloran Bay, ensenada de la costa noroeste de la diminuta isla de Colonsay, es una de las playas más bellas de Escocia.

Kiloran Bay, une anse sur la côte nord-ouest de la petite île Colonsay est l'une des plus belles plages d'Écosse.

Isle of Orsay

NEAR PORTNAHAVEN, ISLAY

The Isle of Orsay faces Port Wemyss at the very north of Islay. The lighthouse was built by Robert Stevenson (1772–1850) in 1825.

Die Insel Orsay liegt vor Port Wemyss, einer Stadt im äußersten Norden der Insel Islay. Der Leuchtturm wurde 1825 von Robert Stevenson (1772–1850) gebaut.

La Isla de Orsay se encuentra frente al Puerto Wemyss en el extremo norte de Islay. El faro fue construido por Robert Stevenson (1772–1850) en el año 1825.

L'île d'Orsay se trouve face à Wemyss au nord de l'île d'Islay. Le phare fut construit par Robert Stevenson (1772–1850) en 1825.

St Ninian's Isle

SHETLAND

St Ninian's Isle is a small island, inhabited only by sheep, that adjoins the south-western coast of mainland Shetland.

St. Ninian ist eine kleine, nur von Schafen bewohnte Insel, die durch einen Dünenstreifen mit der Südwestküste Mainlands, der Hauptinsel der Shetlandinseln, verbunden ist.

La pequeña isla St Ninian está habitada sólo por ovejas y linda con la costa suroeste del archipiélago Shetland.

L'île de St-Ninian est une petite île uniquement habitée par des moutons, qui jouxte la côte sud-ouest du continent Shetland.

Ring of Brodgar

ORKNEY

The remaining 27 stones of this ancient ring rise starkly from the strip of land that lies between Stenness Loch and Harray Loch.

Die noch erhaltenen 27 Steine dieses Ringes ragen aus dem Landstreifen zwischen Loch Stenness und Harray heraus.

Las 27 piedras restantes de este antiguo anillo se levantan imponentemente sobre la franja de tierra que se extiende entre Stenness Loch y Harray Loch.

Les 27 mégalithes restantes de cet ancien cercle se détachent nettement au dessus de l'étroite bande de terre située entre les deux lochs Stenness et Harray.

Yesnaby Sea Stack

ORKNEY

Yesnaby boasts spectacular scenery, including sea stacks formed by the ferocious Atlantic seas, which demonstrate the power and beauty of nature.

Yesnaby bietet beeindruckende Landschaften, etwa durch den stürmischen Atlantik gebildete Felsnadeln, die die Kraft und Schönheit der Natur veranschaulichen.

Yesnaby cuenta con paisajes espectaculares, incluyendo pilares de roca formados por el bravo Mar Atlántico, que demuestran el poder y la belleza de la naturaleza.

Yesnaby offre des paysages spectaculaires, tels les éperons d'érosion marine formés par les vagues violentes de l'Atlantique, témoignant de la puissance et la beauté de la nature.

THE HIGHLANDS

Highland culture is both fascinating and varied. Many things considered to define Scotland are abundant in the Highlands: castles, mountains, lochs, glens, clans, Gaelic, Highland Games, haggis and, of course, the Loch Ness monster.

Die Highland-Kultur ist sowohl faszinierend als auch vielfältig. Viele Dinge, die in unseren Augen Schottland definieren, gibt es in den Highlands: Schlösser, Berge, Seen, Schluchten, Clans, Gälisch, Highland Games, Haggis – und natürlich das Monster von Loch Ness.

La cultura de las Highlands es tan fascinante como variada. Muchos aspectos considerados típicamente escoceses abundan en las Highlands: castillos, montañas, lochs, glens, clanes, el gaélico, los juegos tradicionales de las Highlands, el haggis y, por supuesto, el monstruo del Lago Ness.

La culture des Highlands est à la fois fascinante et variée. Les Highlands comptent plusieurs éléments considérés typiquement écossais: châteaux, montagnes, lacs, vallées, clans, le gaélique, les jeux des Highlands, le plat traditionnel Haggis et bien sûr, le monstre du Loch Ness.

Tarbat Ness

DORNOCH FIRTH, ROSS AND CROMARTY

Tarbat Ness is famed for its lighthouse, which was built in 1830 by Robert Stevenson and at 53 m (174 ft) is the third tallest in Scotland.

Tarbat Ness ist für seinen im Jahr 1830 von Robert Stevenson erbauten Leuchtturm berühmt, der mit 53 Metern der dritthöchste in Schottland ist.

Tarbat Ness es famoso por su faro que, construido en el año 1830 por Robert Stevenson y con 53 metros de altura, es el tercero más alto de Escocia.

Tarbat Ness est célèbre pour son phare qui fut construit en 1830 par Robert Stevenson et est le troisième phare le plus haut d'Écosse avec 53 m de hauteur (174 pieds).

River Torridon

WESTER ROSS

The pretty River Torridon in Wester Ross is only 6 km (4 miles) long and is popular for salmon and trout fishing.

Der idyllische Fluss Torridon in Wester Ross ist nur 6 km lang und bei Lachs- und Forellenfischern sehr beliebt.

El idílico río Torridon de Wester Ross de sólo 6 kilómetros de longitud es popular por la pesca del salmón y la trucha.

La jolie rivière Torridon dans Wester Ross, populaire pour la pêche au saumon et à la truite, fait seulement 6 km (4 miles) de long.

Suilven

NEAR LOCHINVER, SUTHERLAND

Suilven is very popular with climbers. Sometimes called the 'Sugar Loaf', its name actually derives from the Norse 'Pillar Mountain'.

Suilven ist bei Bergsteigern sehr beliebt. Manchmal wird er „Zuckerhut" genannt, sein Name geht jedoch auf den altnordischen „Säulenberg" zurück.

Suilven es muy popular entre los escaladores. Aunque a veces se le denomine 'Pan de Azúcar', su nombre en realidad deriva del escandinavo 'Montaña Pilar'.

Suilven est très populaire auprès des grimpeurs. Parfois appelé le "Pain de Sucre", son nom dérive en fait du norrois "Montagne pilier".

Eilean Donan Castle

DORNIE

Situated on a small island of the same name where three lochs meet, Eilean Donan Castle's setting is particularly picturesque.

Eilean Donan Castle liegt sehr malerisch auf einer kleinen Insel gleichen Namens, bei der drei Meeresbuchten zusammentreffen.

El especialmente pintoresco Castillo Eilean Donan se encuentra situado en una pequeña isla del mismo nombre, en la que se juntan 3 *lochs*.

Situé sur une petite île du même nom où trois *lochs* se rejoignent, le cadre du château d'Eilean Donan est particulièrement pittoresque.

Duncansby Head

NEAR JOHN O'GROATS, CAITHNESS

Duncansby Head is located on the north-eastern tip of the mainland and is in fact slightly further from Land's End than its more famous neighbour.

Duncansby Head liegt an der nordöstlichen Spitze Schottlands und ist von Land's End, dem westlichsten Punkt des britischen Festlandes, weiter entfernt als sein berühmter Nachbar, John o' Groats.

Duncansby Head se encuentra en la punta más al noreste de Escocia continental y está, de hecho, un poco más alejado de Land s End que su vecino más famoso, el pueblo de John O'Groats.

Duncansby Head, situé sur la pointe nord-est du continent, est un peu plus éloigné de Land's End que son voisin plus célèbre, le village de John O'Groats.

Ullapool

LOCH BROOM

Ullapool's origins go back to 1788, when it was designed and built by Thomas Telford (1757–1834) and the British Fisheries Society.

Ullapools Ursprünge gehen auf das Jahr 1788 zurück, als es von Thomas Telford (1757–1834) und der British Fisheries Society (Britische Fischereigesellschaft) entworfen und gebaut wurde.

Los orígenes de Ullapool se remontan al año 1788, cuando fue diseñado y construido por Thomas Telford (1757–1834) y la British Fisheries Society ('Sociedad Británica para la Pesca').

Les origines du village d'Ullapool, conçu et construit par Thomas Telford (1757–1834) et la Société Britannique de Pêche, remontent à 1788.

Urquhart Castle

LOCH NESS

Urquhart Castle, located on the banks of Loch Ness, dates from around 1230 and was donated to the National Trust for Scotland in 2003.

Urquhart Castle liegt am Ufer des Loch Ness, wurde um 1230 erbaut und ist seit 2003 im Besitz des National Trust for Scotland.

El Castillo Urquhart, situado en la orilla del Lago Ness, es aproximadamente del año 1230 y fue donado al National Trust for Scotland (Patrimonio Nacional de Escocia) en el año 2003.

Le château de Urquhart, situé sur les rives du Loch Ness, date des environs de 1230 et fut donné au National Trust for Scotland en 2003 ("société pour la conservation des Sites et Monuments d'Écosse").

Loch Ewe

NEAR COVE, POOLEWE

Pictured above at sunset, the peninsula of Cove glides around one side of the beautiful Loch Ewe, at the centre of which is the Isle of Ewe.

Die bei Sonnenuntergang abgebildete Halbinsel Cove (oben) liegt auf einer Seite des schönen Loch Ewe, in dessen Mitte sich die Insel Ewe befindet.

Imagen superior tomada a la puesta de sol. La península de Cove se asienta junto al hermoso Loch Ewe, en cuyo centro se encuentra la isla de Ewe.

Sur la photo ci-dessus au coucher du soleil, la presqu'île de Cove s'avance le long d'un coté du magnifique Loch Ewe, au centre duquel se trouve l'île d'Ewe.

Plockton

NEAR KYLE OF LOCHALSH

Snuggling up to the shore of Loch Carron, Plockton (left) is a popular tourist spot, with pretty cottages curving around the harbour.

Plockton (links) schmiegt sich an das Ufer des Loch Carron und ist mit seinen hübschen, am Hafen gelegenen Cottages ein beliebter Touristenort.

Arrimándose a la orilla de Loch Carron, Plockton (foto izquierda) es un destino turístico popular, con cottages preciosos junto al puerto

Blotti au bord du Loch Carron, Plockton (à gauche), avec ses jolies maisonettes assises le long du port, est un lieu touristique très populaire.

Loch Poulary

GLEN GARRY

At only 3 km (2 miles) long, Loch Poulary was created during the damming of the River Garry as part of the Garry-Moriston Hydro-Electric Scheme.

Loch Poulary, der nur 3 km lang ist, ist durch die Stauung des Flusses Garry, einer Phase des Garry-Moriston-Hydroelektrizitäts-programms, entstanden.

De sólo 3 km de longitud, Loch Poulary fue creado durante la construcción de presas en el río Garry como parte del Proyecto Hidroeléctrico Garry-Moriston.

Avec seulement 3 km de long (2 miles), Loch Poulary fut créé pendant la construction du barrage de la rivière Garry dans le cadre du projet hydroélectrique Garry-Moriston.

Mallaig

LOCHABER

Once one of Europe's busiest herring ports, Mallaig continues to be at the centre of the Scottish fishing industry, specialising in prawns and seafood.

Mallaig, früher eines der Zentren der Heringsfischerei Europas, ist heute auf den Fang von Garnelen und Meeresfrüchte spezialisiert und damit auch weiterhin Mittelpunkt der schottischen Fischerei.

Mallaig, uno de los puertos de arenque más activos de Europa en el pasado, continúa ocupando el centro de la industria escocesa de la pesca especializándose en langostinos y marisco.

Jadis un des ports de pêche au hareng les plus fréquentés d'Europe, Mallaig reste encore au centre de l'industrie écossaise de la pêche et se spécialise dans les crevettes et les fruits de mer.

Inverness

Inverness, on the River Ness, was granted city status by the Queen in December 2000 and is the unofficial Capital of the Highlands.

Inverness, die am Fluss Ness gelegene inoffizielle Hauptstadt des Hochlandes, wurde im Dezember 2000 von der Königin zur Stadt erhoben.

A Inverness, junto al río Ness, se le concedió el título de ciudad por la Reina en diciembre de 2000 y es la capital 'no oficial' de las Highlands.('Tierras Altas')

Inverness, sur la rivière Ness, s'est vu accorder le statut de ville par la Reine en Décembre 2000, et est la capitale officieuse des Highlands (Hautes Terres).

Five Sisters of Kintail

GLEN SHIEL

The mountains that rise above Glen Shiel are known as the Five Sisters of Kintail, after a legend about the King of Kintail's daughters.

Die Berge, die sich über Glen Shiel erheben, sind nach einer Legende über König Kintails Töchter als die „Fünf Schwestern von Kintail" bekannt.

Las montañas que se elevan por encima de Glen Shiel son conocidas como 'Las cinco hijas de Kintail', según una leyenda sobre las hijas del Rey de Kintail.

Les montagnes s'élevant au-dessus de Glen Shiel sont connues sous le nom des Cinq Soeurs de Kintail d'après une légende des filles du roi de Kintail.

Corpach and Ben Nevis

NEAR FORT WILLIAM

One of the best views of Ben Nevis is from the village of Corpach (previous pages), as the mountain soars above Fort William.

Eine der besten Ansichten von Ben Nevis ist vom Dorf Corpach (vorherige Seiten) aus, wo sich der Berg über Fort William erhebt.

Desde el pueblo de Corpach se obtiene una de las mejores vistas sobre Ben Nevis (doble página anterior), al elevarse la montaña por encima de Fort William.

Depuis le village de Corpach (pages précédentes), on bénéficie d'une des meilleures vues du Ben Nevis, là où la montagne s'élève au-dessus de Fort William.

Glen Coe

Glen Coe – thought to mean 'narrow glen' or 'glen of weeping' – is one of the most striking and majestic places in Scotland.

Glen Coe – was „enge Schlucht" oder „Tal des Weinens" bedeuten könnte – ist eine der eindrucksvollsten und großartigsten Gegenden Schottlands.

Glen Coe – se cree que significa 'valle estrecho' o 'valle del llanto' – es uno de los lugares más asombrosos y majestuosos de Escocia.

Glen Coe – qui signifierait 'étroit vallon' ou 'vallée des larmes'– est l'un des endroits les plus beaux et majestueux de l'Écosse.

Glenfinnan Monument

LOCH SHIEL

The Glenfinnan Monument was erected in 1815 to commemorate the clansmen who fought and died in honour of the exiled Stuarts.

Das Glenfinnan Monument wurde 1815 im Gedenken an die Mitglieder der Clans errichtet, die für die im Exil lebenden Stuarts gekämpft haben und gestorben sind.

El Monumento Glenfinnan fue erigido en el año 1815 para conmemorar a los miembros del clan que lucharon y murieron en honor de los Estuardos exiliados.

Le monument Glenfinnan fut érigé en 1815 pour commémorer les hommes du clan qui ont combattu et sont morts en l'honneur des Stuarts exilés.

Rannoch Moor

LOCHABER AND PERTH AND KINROSS

Created 20,000 years ago by glaciers, Rannoch Moor (above) is one of the last truly wild places in Scotland and spans 5,200 hectares (12,800 acres).

Das vor 20 000 Jahren von Gletschern geformte Rannoch Moor (oben) ist eine der letzten Wildnisse in Schottland und umfasst 5200 Hektar.

Creado hace 20.000 años por glaciares, Rannoch Moor que abarca unas 5.200 hectáreas (foto superior), es uno de los últimos lugares verdaderamente salvajes de Escocia.

Rannoch Moor (ci-dessus) créé par des glaciers il y a 20.000 ans, est l'un des derniers endroits vraiment sauvages en Écosse et s'étend sur 5.200 hectares (12,800 acres).

Eas Chia-aig Falls

NEAR CLUNES, LOCH LOCHY

The spectacular Eas Chia-aig Falls (left) are located at the end of a wooded pass, romantically named Mile Dorcha ('dark mile').

Die spektakulären Wasserfälle Eas Chia-aig (links) befinden sich am Ende eines Waldweges mit dem romantischen Namen Mile Dorcha („Dunkle Meile").

Las espectaculares cataratas Eas Chia-aig (foto izquierda) se encuentran al final de un paso arbolado, románticamente llamado Mile Dorcha ('la milla oscura')

Les chutes spectaculaires d'Eas Chia-aig (à gauche) sont situées à l'extrémité d'un sentier boisé, au nom romantique de Mile Dorcha ("mile sombre").

GRAMPIAN AND ABERDEEN

The Grampian Highlands deserve their reputation as Scotland's 'castle country' with more than 70 castles, as well as a multitude of stone circles and hill forts. Meanwhile, Aberdeen is the undisputed capital of the region.

Die Grampian Highlands verdanken ihren Ruf als Schottlands „Land der Schlösser" mehr als 70 Burgen und Schlössern. Hier gibt es auch zahlreiche Steinkreise und Hügelfestungen. Aberdeen ist die unangefochtene Hauptstadt der Region.

Las Highlands ('Tierras Altas') de Grampian se merecen su reputación de 'país de los castillos' de Escocia por sus más de 70 castillos, así como sus círculos de piedra y fortines. Aberdeen es la capital indiscutible de la región.

Les Grampian Highlands ("Hautes-Terre") méritent leur réputation de "région de châteaux" d'Écosse avec plus de 70 châteaux, une multitude de cercles de pierres magiques et des forts dominant leurs collines. Aberdeen est considérée comme la capitale incontestée de la région.

Union Street
ABERDEEN

The austere granite buildings of Aberdeen's Union Street (above) include the Music Hall, the National Bank of Scotland and the Palace Hotel.

▬ Zu den nüchternen Granitgebäuden der Union Street in Aberdeen (oben) zählen die Music Hall, die National Bank of Scotland und das Palace Hotel.

▬ Los edificios austeros de granito de Union Street de Aberdeen (foto superior) incluyen el Palacio de la Música, el Banco Nacional de Escocia y el Hotel Palace.

▮▮ Des bâtiments de granit austères tels le Music Hall, National Bank of Scotland et Palace Hotel sont situés sur la Union Street à Aberdeen (ci-dessus).

Aberdeen Harbour
ABERDEEN

Aberdeen Harbour (left) is the principal port in northern Scotland, handling around five million tonnes of cargo annually.

▬ Aberdeen Harbour (links) ist der wichtigste Hafen Nordschottlands, in dem jährlich rund fünf Millionen Tonnen Fracht umgesetzt werden.

▬ El Puerto de Aberdeen (foto izquierda), principal puerto del norte de Escocia, comercia en torno a 5 millones de toneladas de cargamento al año.

▮▮ La rade d'Aberdeen (à gauche), principal port du nord de l'Écosse, gère environ cinq millions de tonnes de marchandises par an.

Crathes Castle

ABERDEENSHIRE

Crathes Castle is one of the best-loved castles in Scotland and combines a fairy-tale exterior with sumptuous décor and impressive gardens.

Crathes Castle ist mit seiner märchenhaften Fassade, seinem üppigem Dekor und den beeindruckenden Gärten eines der beliebtesten Schlösser in Schottland.

El Castillo Crathes es uno de los castillos más apreciados de Escocia que combina un exterior estilo 'cuento de hadas' con una decoración suntuosa y jardines impresionantes.

Le château de Crathes est l'un des plus appréciés d'Écosse pour son extérieur de conte de fées, son décor somptueux et ses magnifiques jardins.

Dunnottar Castle

NEAR STONEHAVEN, ABERDEENSHIRE

Dunnottar Castle dates back to the late 400s and is most famous for the unsuccessful raid there in 1652 by Oliver Cromwell (1599–1658).

Dunnottar Castle stammt aus dem späten 4. Jahrhundert und ist durch Oliver Cromwells (1599–1658) fehlgeschlagenen Überfall im Jahr 1652 berühmt geworden.

El Castillo Dunnottar se remonta a finales de los años 400 y es famoso sobre todo por el asalto infructuoso que dirigió Oliver Cromwell (1599–1658) en el año 1652.

Le Château de Dunnottar remonte à la fin des années 400 et fut rendu célèbre par le raid manqué d'Oliver Cromwell (1599–1658) sur ce lieu en 1652.

River Dee

River Dee flows for 140 km (90 miles) from the Cairngorm mountains through Royal Deeside, reaching the North Sea at Aberdeen.

Der Fluss Dee, dessen oberer Abschnitt Royal Deeside genannt wird, entspringt in den Cairngorm Mountains und erreicht nach 140 km in Aberdeen die Nordsee.

El río Dee recorre unos 140 km desde las montañas Cairngorm y a través de Royal Deeside hasta alcanzar el Mar del Norte en Aberdeen.

La rivière Dee coule sur 140 kms (90 miles) depuis les montagnes de Cairngorm en passant par Royal Deeside avant de rejoindre la Mer du Nord à Aberdeen.

Castle Fraser

Work began on the imposing Castle Fraser in 1575 under the 6th laird, Michael Fraser, and the building was completed in 1636.

Die Arbeiten am imposanten Castle Fraser begannen im Jahr 1575 unter Aufsicht des 6. Laird, Michael Fraser. Das Gebäude wurde 1636 fertiggestellt.

La construcción del imponente Castillo Fraser comenzó en el año 1575 bajo el 6° *laird*, Michael Fraser, y el edificio se completó en el año 1636.

Les travaux de cet imposant château commencèrent en 1575 sous le 6ème *laird*, Michael Fraser, et furent achevés en 1636.

Stonehaven

ABERDEENSHIRE

Stonehaven is situated 24 km (15 miles) south of Aberdeen. Its charming Old Town and harbour are popular with tourists.

Stonehaven liegt 24 km südlich von Aberdeen. Die charmante Altstadt und der Hafen sind bei Touristen sehr beliebt.

Stonehaven está situado a 24 km al sur de Aberdeen. Su encantador casco antiguo y puerto son populares entre los turistas.

Stonehaven est situé à 24 km (15 miles) au sud d'Aberdeen. Sa vieille ville charmante et son port sont très populaires auprès des touristes.

Pennan

ABERDEENSHIRE

Pennan consists of only one street of white cottages and is famous
for being the location of the film *Local Hero* (1983).

 Pennan besteht nur aus einer Straße mit weiß getünchten
Cottages und ist als Drehort des Films *Local Hero* (1983) berühmt.

 Pennan consta de una sola calle de casitas blancas y es famoso
por ser donde se rodó la película *Local Hero* (1983).

 Le village de Pennan avec son unique rue aux cottages
peints en blanc, est célèbre pour avoir été le lieu de tournage du
film *Local Hero* (1983).

Craigievar Castle

NEAR BALLATER

Built in the early seventeenth century, Craigievar Castle was home to
the Forbes family and saw guests such as Queen Victoria (1819–1901).

 Das im frühen 17. Jahrhundert erbaute Craigievar Castle war
der Wohnsitz der Familie Forbes und hieß Gäste wie Königin Victoria
(1819–1901) willkommen.

 Construido a principios del siglo XVII, el Castillo Craigievar fue
el hogar de la familia Forbes y vio pasar a huéspedes tales como la
Reina Victoria (1819–1901).

 Construit au début du XVIIème siècle, le château de Craigievar
fut la demeure de la famille Forbes et reçut des invités tels que la
reine Victoria (1819–1901).

Covesea Lighthouse

LOSSIEMOUTH, MORAY

Covesea Lighthouse, built in 1844 by Alan Stevenson (1807–65), is 5 m (18 ft) tall and is now fully automated.

Der Leuchtturm Covesea wurde 1844 von Alan Stevenson (1807–1865) erbaut. Er ist 5 Meter hoch und jetzt vollständig automatisiert.

Construido en el año 1844 por Alan Stevenson (1807–65) y de 5 metros de altura, el Faro de Covesea se encuentra en la actualidad completamente automatizado.

Le phare de Covesea, construit en 1844 par Alan Stevenson (1807–65) fait 5 m de hauteur (18 pieds) et est maintenant entièrement automatisé.

Bow Fiddle Rock

PORTNOCKIE, MORAY

Bow Fiddle Rock, so-called because its arch resembles a violin bow, is a stunning natural arch made of quartzite rocks.

Bow Fiddle Rock ist ein atemberaubender natürlicher Felsbogen aus Quarz, der deshalb so heißt, weil er einem Geigenbogen ähnelt.

El Bow Fiddle Rock, llamado así debido a que su forma se asemeja a un arco de violín, es un impresionante arco natural formado por piedras de cuarcita.

Bow Fiddle Rock, nommé ainsi pour sa forme d'archet de violon, est une arche naturelle magnifique en roche de quartz.

Elgin Cathedral

ELGIN, MORAY

One of the most magnificent ruins in Scotland, Elgin Cathedral dates back to the 1200s and is still architecturally awe-inspiring.

Die Elgin Cathedral, eine der schönsten Ruinen Schottlands, wurde im 13. Jahrhundert erbaut und ist architektonisch immer noch beeindruckend.

Una de las ruinas más espectaculares de Escocia, La Catedral Elgin que se remonta al siglo XIII, sigue siendo de una arquitectura impresionante.

La Cathédrale d'Elgin, une merveille architecturale datant des années 1200, est un des vestiges les plus grandioses d'Écosse.

Findochty

MORAY

The focus of Findochty village is its harbour, known as Crooked Haven, with a series of pretty cottages that follow its curve.

Der Mittelpunkt des Dorfes Findochty ist sein Hafen, der Crooked Haven, an dessen gekrümmter Küstenlinie eine Reihe hübscher Cottages liegt.

El punto de encuentro del pueblo de Findochty es su puerto, conocido como Crooked Haven ('refugio torcido'), y los cottages que lo bordean.

L'attrait du village de Findochty, connu sous le nom de "Crooked Haven" (havre crochu), réside dans son port et ses jolis cottages entourant la rade.

CENTRAL SCOTLAND

Central Scotland has a varied landscape, the most well-known
feature of which is probably the stunning Loch Lomond.
At the region's heart is Stirling, with its famous castle,
while to the north is Rob Roy country.

Central Schottland bietet eine abwechslungsreiche Landschaft, am
bekanntesten ist wohl der wunderschöne Loch Lomond. Im Herzen
der Region liegt Stirling mit seinem berühmten Schloss, während sich
im Norden das Land von Rob Roy befindet.

Escocia Central tiene un paisaje variado cuyo rasgo más conocido
es probablemente el sensacional Loch Lomond. En el corazón
de la región está Stirling, con su famoso castillo, y
más al norte se encuentra 'la tierra' Rob Roy.

Le Centre de l'Écosse possède un paysage très varié dont
l'extraordinaire Loch Lomond est probablement la représentation la
plus significative. Au coeur de la région se trouvent Stirling et son
célèbre château, et plus au nord le pays de Rob Roy.

Queen's View

LOCH TUMMEL, PERTH AND KINROSS

Situated just outside Pitlochry, Queen's View is a breathtaking panorama of Loch Tummel and the surrounding mountain scenery.

Außerhalb von Pitlochry gelegen bietet Queen's View, der „Ausblick der Königin", ein atemberaubendes Panorama des Loch Tummel und der umliegenden Bergwelt.

Situado justo a las afueras de Pitlochry, Queen s View ofrece un impresionante panorama de Loch Tummel y de las montañas que lo rodean.

Situé à la sortie de Pitlochry, Queen's View offre un panorama époustouflant du Loch Tummel et des montagnes environnantes.

Kenmore

NEAR ABERFELDY, PERTH AND KINROSS

Idyllically situated on an outlet at the eastern end of Loch Tay, Kenmore is a beautiful village of whitewashed cottages.

Kenmore ist ein hübsches Dorf mit weiß getünchten Häusern, das idyllisch am östlichen Ende des Loch Tay liegt.

Idílicamente situado en el extremo este de Loch Tay, Kenmore es un precioso pueblo de casitas encaladas.

Idylliquement situé dans une anse à l'extrémité Est du Loch Tay, Kenmore est un beau village de maisons blanchies à la chaux.

Scone Palace

PERTH AND KINROSS

Once the crowning place for the Kings of Scots, Scone Palace was also the setting for William Shakespeare's (1564–1616) *Macbeth*.

Scone Palace, früher die Krönungsstätte der schottischen Könige, war auch der Schauplatz von William Shakespeares (1564–1616) *Macbeth*.

El que fue el lugar de coronación de los Reyes de Escocia, Scone Palace fue también el escenario de *Macbeth* de William Shakespeare (1564–1616).

Autrefois le lieu de couronnement des Rois écossais, Scone Place servit aussi de décor pour *Macbeth* de William Shakespeare (1564–1616).

Falls of Dochart

KILLIN, STIRLING

The Falls of Dochart form one of the most scenic sections of the River Dochart as they rush under the bridge at the village of Killin.

Die Wasserfälle von Dochart, über die im Dorf Killin eine Brücke führt, sind einer der landschaftlich reizvollsten Abschnitte des Flusses Dochart.

Las Cascadas de Dochart forman una de las secciones más espectaculares del río Dochart a su paso por el puente del pueblo de Killin.

Les chutes de Dochart dévalant sous le pont du village de Killin, sont un des endroits les plus pittoresques de la rivière Dochart.

Loch Ard, Aberfoyle

THE TROSSACHS, STIRLING

Loch Ard (previous pages) is famously described by Sir Walter Scott (1771–1832) in his novel *Rob Roy* as 'an enchanting sheet of water'.

Der Loch Ard (vorherige Seiten) wurde von Sir Walter Scott (1771–1832) in seinem Roman *Rob Roy* als „eine bezaubernde Wasserfläche" beschrieben.

Loch Ard (doble página anterior) es famosamente descrito por Sir Walter Scott (1771–1832) en su novela *Rob Roy* como 'una encantadora sábana de agua'.

Loch Ard (pages précédentes) fut rendu célèbre dans le roman *Rob Roy* de Sir Walter Scott (1771–1832) où il le décrit comme 'une nappe d'eau enchanteresse'.

Old Stirling Bridge and Wallace Monument

STIRLING

The Battle of Stirling Bridge took place on 11 September 1297, when Sir William Wallace (1272–1305) and his men triumphantly fought the English.

In der Schlacht von Stirling Bridge am 11. September 1297 besiegten Sir William Wallace (1272–1305) und seine Männer die Engländer.

La batalla de Stirling Bridge tuvo lugar el 11 de Septiembre de 1297, cuando Sir William Wallace (1272–1305) y sus hombres vencieron a los ingleses.

Sir William Wallace (1272–1305) et ses hommes ont combattu victorieusement les Anglais lors de la bataille du pont de Stirling le 11 Septembre 1297.

Stirling Castle

STIRLING

Stirling Castle, now cared for by Historic Scotland, stands proud on crags of volcanic rock and can be seen for miles around.

Stirling Castle, das heute von Historic Scotland verwaltet wird, steht stolz auf vulkanischen Felsen und ist nach allen Seiten hin kilometerweit sichtbar.

El Castillo De Stirling, en la actualidad bajo gestión de Historic Scotland ('Escocia Histórica'), se alza orgulloso sobre riscos de piedra volcánica y es visible a kilómetros de distancia.

Le château de Stirling, perché en haut d'un rocher volcanique, est de nos jours entretenu par l'Historic Scotland (agence écossaise des monuments historiques) et peut être vu à des kilomètres à la ronde.

Loch Lomond

ARGYLL AND BUTE

Loch Lomond is the largest freshwater loch in the UK at 39 km (24 miles) long, 8 km (5 miles) wide and at its deepest 183 m (600 ft) deep.

Loch Lomond ist mit seinen 39 Kilometern Länge, 8 Kilometern Breite und bis zu 183 Metern Tiefe der größte See im Vereinigten Königreich.

Loch Lomond es el *loch* de agua dulce más grande del Reino Unido con sus 39 km de largo, 8 km de ancho y, en su punto más hondo, 183 metros de profundidad.

Loch Lomond est le plus grand Loch d'eau douce au Royaume-Uni avec 39 km (24 miles) de long, 8 km (5 miles) de large et une profondeur maximale de 183 m (600 pieds).

City Square

DUNDEE CITY CENTRE, DUNDEE

Dundee's City Square lies at the heart of the city and is home to the City Chambers and the impressive, Doric-columned Caird Hall.

Auf Dundees City Square im Herzen der Stadt finden sich die City Chambers und die beeindruckende Caird Hall mit ihren dorischen Säulen.

La Plaza de la Ciudad, situada en pleno centro de Dundee, está rodeada por las City Chambers ('Salas de la Ciudad') y el impresionante Caird Hall ('Auditorio Caird') de columnas dóricas.

Sur la place de Dundee se trouvent la City Chambers et l'imposant Caird Hall (salle de concert) aux colonnes doriques.

Loch Katrine

THE TROSSACHS

Sir Walter Scott's first major work, *The Lady of the Lake*, describes
scenery inspired by the landscape around Loch Katrine.

Sir Walter Scotts erstes bedeutendes Werk, *The Lady of the
Lake*, beschreibt einen Schauplatz, der durch die Landschaft rund um
Loch Katrine inspiriert war.

La primera gran obra del Sir Walter Scott, *The Lady of the Lake*
('*La Dama del Lago*'), describe escenarios inspirados en el paisaje de
los alrededores de Loch Katrine.

La première oeuvre d'importance de Sir Walter Scott, *The Lady
of the Lake*, décrit un paysage des alentours de Loch Katrine.

The Falkirk Wheel

FALKIRK

The magnificent Falkirk Wheel is the world's first and only rotating
boat lift, and was opened by the Queen in May 2002.

Das beeindruckende Falkirk Wheel ist weltweit das erste und
einzige rotierende Schiffshebewerk und wurde im Mai 2002 von der
Königin eröffnet.

La magnífica 'Rueda de Falkirk' es el primer y único ascensor
rotativo para barcos del mundo y fue inaugurado por la Reina
en mayo de 2002.

La roue de Falkirk, inaugurée par la Reine en mai 2002,
est le premier et le seul ascenseur à bateaux rotatif au monde.

EDINBURGH, LOTHIAN AND FIFE

In this region lies the most famous of all Scottish castles,
Edinburgh Castle, the architectural wonder of the Forth Rail Bridge
and St Andrews, one of the most prestigious university
and golfing towns in the country.

In dieser Region liegen die berühmteste schottische Burg,
Edinburgh Castle, das architektonische Wunder der Forth Rail Bridge
und St Andrews, eine der renommiertesten Universitäts-
und Golfstädte des Landes.

En esta región se encuentra el más famoso de todos los castillos
escoceses, el Castillo de Edimburgo, la maravilla arquitectónica del
Puente de Forth y St Andrews, que es una de las universidades y
zonas de golf más prestigiosas del país.

Dans cette région se trouvent le plus célèbre de tous les châteaux
écossais, le château d'Edinburgh, la merveille architecturale du Pont
du Forth et St Andrews qui abrite une des universités les plus
réputées du pays et surtout des parcours de golf prestigieux.

Forth Rail Bridge

NEAR EDINBURGH, LOTHIAN

Designed by Sir Benjamin Baker (1840–1907) and Sir John Fowler (1817–98), the Forth Rail Bridge took seven years to build.

Es hat sieben Jahre gedauert, die von Sir Benjamin Baker (1840–1907) und Sir John Fowler (1817–1898) entworfene Forth Rail Bridge zu bauen.

Diseñado por Sir Benjamin Baker (1840–1907) y Sir John Fowler (1817–98), el Puente de Forth se construyó en siete años.

Il a fallu sept ans pour construire le pont du Forth qui fut conçu par Sir Benjamin Baker (1840–1907) et Sir John Fowler (1817–98).

Edinburgh Military Tattoo

EDINBURGH

Edinburgh's Military Tattoo commands an annual audience of around 217,000 and boasts performances from over 30 countries.

Edinburgh Military Tattoo, das größte Musikfestival Schottlands, zieht jährlich rund 217 000 Zuseher an und bietet Aufführungen aus über 30 Ländern an.

El festival *'Military Tattoo'* de Edimburgo recibe una audiencia anual de unas 217.000 personas y cuenta con actuaciones de más de 30 países.

Le Festival Tattoo Militaire d'Édinburgh reçoit un public annuel de près de 217.000 personnes et propose des spectacles prestigieux originaires de plus de 30 pays.

The Palace of Holyroodhouse

EDINBURGH

The Palace of Holyroodhouse, at the edge of Holyrood Park, is the official residence of Her Majesty the Queen in Scotland.

Der am Rande des Holyrood Park gelegene Palace of Holyrood ist die offizielle Residenz Ihrer Majestät der Königin von Schottland.

El Palacio de Holyroodhouse, situado en el borde de Holyrood Park, es la residencia oficial de Su Majestad la Reina en Escocia.

Le Palais de Holyroodhouse, à la lisière du parc Holyrood, est la résidence officielle de Sa Majesté la Reine en Écosse.

Scottish Parliament Building (Office Window)

EDINBURGH

Designed by Enric Miralles (1955–2000), the striking and controversial Scottish Parliament Building signifies the rebirth of a nation.

Das markante und kontroverse, von Enric Miralles (1955–2000) entworfene schottische Parlamentsgebäude symbolisiert die Wiedergeburt einer Nation.

Diseñado por el catalán Enric Miralles (1955–2000), el asombroso y controvertido Edificio del Parlamento Escocés simboliza el renacimiento de una nación.

Conçu par Enric Miralles (1955–2000), l'étonnant et controversé édifice du Parlement illustre la renaissance de la nation écossaise.

The Scott Monument

EDINBURGH

This Gothic monument in Princes Street Gardens was built in 1846 to commemorate Edinburgh's literary son, Sir Walter Scott.

Dieses gotische Bauwerk in den Princes Street Gardens wurde 1846 zum Gedenken an den literarischen Sohn Edinburghs, Sir Walter Scott, gebaut.

Este monumento gótico en Princes Street Gardens fue construido en 1816 para conmemorar al hijo literario de Edimburgo, Sir Walter Scott.

Ce monument gothique dans Princes Street Gardens fut édifié en 1846 en l'honneur de Sir Walter Scott, fils littéraire d'Édinburgh.

Edinburgh Castle

EDINBURGH

Rising from an ancient volcanic plug, Edinburgh's majestic castle looms over the capital city from a height of 80 m (262 ft).

Edinburghs majestätische Burg, die auf einem Basaltkegel eines erloschenen Vulkans erbaut wurde, thront auf einer Höhe von 80 Metern über der Hauptstadt.

Alzándose sobre una roca de origen volcánico, el majestuoso Castillo de Edimburgo se cierne sobre la capital desde una altura de 80 metros.

Erigé sur un rocher d'origine volcanique, le majestueux château d' Edinburgh surplombe la ville du haut de ses 80 m (262 pieds).

John Knox's House

EDINBURGH

It is not known whether Protestant reformer John Knox (c. 1514–72) ever lived here, but it is now a museum to Knox and the Reformation.

Man weiß nicht, ob der protestantische Reformator John Knox (um 1514–1572) je in diesem Haus gelebt hat, das heute ein Museum über ihn und die Reformation beherbergt.

No se sabe si el reformador protestante John Knox (1514–72) llegó a vivir en esta casa alguna vez, pero ahora es un museo sobre él y la Reforma.

John Knox (c.1514–72) aurait séjourné dans cette maison transformée en musée consacré à son oeuvre et au mouvement réformateur.

Near Cupar

FIFE

In this scene, near the historic town of Cupar, miles of bright yellow rapeseed fields liven up the traditional landscape.

Auf diesem Bild, in der Nähe der historischen Stadt Cupar aufgenommen, beleben leuchtend gelbe Rapsfelder kilometerweit die traditionelle Landschaft.

En este paisaje cerca del pueblo histórico de Cupar, kilómetros de campos brillantes de colza amarilla animan el paisaje tradicional.

Dans cette scène, près de la ville historique de Cupar, des kilomètres de champs de colza jaune vif colorent ce paysage traditionnel.

Elie

FIFE

The seaside resort of Elie has been popular with families since Victorian times, when the village became accessible by steamer and train.

In Badeort Elie ist seit viktorianischen Zeiten bei Familien beliebt, als das Dorf mit Dampfschiff und Bahn erreicht werden konnte.

El centro turístico costero de Elie ha sido popular entre familias desde la época victoriana, cuando el pueblo se hizo accesible por barco de vapor y tren.

Depuis l'époque victorienne, quand le village est devenu accessible par bateau et par train, la station balnéaire d'Elie est devenue une destination populaire pour les familles.

St Andrews (Cathedral Ruins)

FIFE

St Andrews is home to a world-renowned golf course, a top university, St Andrews Castle and the medieval ruins of the Cathedral.

In St Andrews befinden sich ein weltweit bekannter Golfplatz, eine erstklassige Universität, das St Andrews Castle und die mittelalterlichen Ruinen der Kathedrale.

St Andrews ofrece un campo de golf conocido a nivel mundial, una universidad de primera clase, el Castillo de St Andrews y las ruinas medievales de la catedral.

St Andrews possède un terrain de golf de renommée mondiale, une université réputée, le chateau St Andrews et les ruines médiévales de la cathédrale.

Crail

FIFE

Situated 16 km (10 miles) south-east of St Andrews, Crail was authorised as a royal burgh by King Robert the Bruce (1274–1329) in 1310.

Crail, 16 km südöstlich von St Andrews, wurde im Jahr 1310 von König Robert the Bruce (1274–1329) als königliche Burg anerkannt.

Situado a 16 km al sureste de St Andrews, Crail fue decretado 'villa real' por el Rey Robert the Bruce (1274–1329) allá por el año 1310.

Le roi Robert le Bruce (1274–1329) accorda à Crail, situé à 16 km (10 miles) au sud-est de St Andrews, le statut de ville royale en 1310.

Preston Mill

EAST LOTHIAN

The eighteenth-century Preston Mill sits at the edge of the River Tyne and houses an exhibition demonstrating its milling machinery.

Die aus dem 18. Jahrhundert stammende Wassermühle in Preston liegt am Ufer des Flusses Tyne und beherbergt eine Ausstellung über ihre Mühlentechnik.

El Molino Preston del siglo XVIII y que se halla junto al río Tyne, alberga una exposición que muestra su maquinaria de molinería.

Preston Mill (Le Moulin de Preston) du XVIIIème siècle en bordure de la rivière Tyne abrite une exposition sur le fonctionnement de ses machines.

GLASGOW, CLYDE VALLEY AND ARGYLL

Glasgow, Scotland's biggest city, is illustrated beautifully here, with stunning photography of the varied architecture and the River Clyde, as well as nearby villages and buildings of interest.

Glasgow, Schottlands größte Stadt, ist hier anhand eindrucksvoller Fotografien von seiner vielfältigen Architektur und dem Fluss Clyde sowie von nahegelegenen Dörfern und interessanten Gebäuden dargestellt.

Glasgow, la ciudad más grande de Escocia, está hermosamente ilustrada aquí mediante fotografías impresionantes de su variada arquitectura y del río Clyde, así como de pueblos cercanos y de edificios de interés.

Glasgow, la plus grande ville d'Écosse, est ici magnifiquement illustrée par des photographies spectaculaires de son architecture variée, de la rivière Clyde, ainsi que des villages et des monuments avoisinants de grand intérêt.

River Clyde

GLASGOW

The River Clyde was formerly the hub of Glasgow's engineering and shipbuilding industries; now luxury flats dominate its banks.

Der Fluss Clyde war früher das Zentrum der Maschinenbau- und Schiffsbauindustrie in Glasgow, doch jetzt dominieren Luxuswohnungen seine Ufer.

El río Clyde, que fue centro ingeniero y naval de Glasgow, ofrece en la actualidad pisos de lujo en sus márgenes.

De nos jours, des appartements de luxe dominent les bords de la rivière Clyde, autrefois le centre d'industrie d'équipement et de construction navale de Glasgow.

Glasgow University from Kelvingrove Park

GLASGOW

The spire of Glasgow University is visible from many parts of the city and is a reminder of Glasgow's academic heritage.

Der Turm der Universität von Glasgow ist von vielen Stadtteilen aus sichtbar und erinnert an das akademische Erbe Glasgows.

La torre de la Universidad de Glasgow se puede ver desde muchas partes de la ciudad y es un recordatorio del patrimonio académico de Glasgow.

La flèche de l'Université de Glasgow, visible depuis de nombreux endroits de la ville, est un symbole du patrimoine académique de la ville.

George Square

GLASGOW

George Square lies in the centre of Glasgow and boasts the famous and architecturally stunning City Chambers, built in 1888.

Der George Square liegt im Zentrum von Glasgow. Hier finden sich die bekannten und architektonisch beeindruckenden City Chambers, die 1888 erbaut wurden.

La Plaza George yace en el centro de Glasgow y cuenta con las famosas y estructuralmente impresionantes City Chambers ('Salas de la ciudad'), construidas en 1888.

Au centre de Glasgow, sur (la place) George Square, se dresse le bâtiment célèbre et extravagant de City Chambers, construit en 1888.

Kelvingrove Art Gallery and Museum

GLASGOW

Kelvingrove Art Gallery and Museum is Glasgow's largest gallery and features works by the Old Masters as well as by Scottish artists.

Kelvingrove Art Gallery and Museum ist Glasgows größtes Kunstmuseum und umfasst sowohl Werke von alten Meistern als auch von schottischen Künstlern.

La Galería y Museo de Arte Kelvingrove es la galería más grande de Glasgow y cuenta con obras tanto de los Antiguos Maestros como de artistas escoceses.

La galerie d'art et musée de Kelvingrove, la plus grande de Glasgow, expose les oeuvres des grands Maîtres de la peinture classique, aussi bien que des artistes écossais.

Oban

ARGYLL AND BUTE

Translating from Gaelic as 'little bay', Oban is a very busy port, ferrying thousands of visitors annually to the nearby islands.

Oban, aus dem Gälischen für „kleine Bucht", ist eine sehr verkehrsreiche Hafenstadt, von der aus jährlich Tausende von Besuchern zu den nahegelegenen Inseln übersetzen.

Traducido del gaélico como 'pequeña bahía', Oban es un puerto muy activo que transporta cada año a miles de visitantes hacía las islas locales.

Signifiant "petite baie" en gaélique, Oban est un port très fréquenté, transportant chaque année des milliers de visiteurs vers les îles voisines.

Castle Stalker

APPIN, LOCH LINNHE, ARGYLL AND BUTE

Built in 1540, Castle Stalker is a four-storey tower house and is one of the best-preserved medieval castles in western Scotland.

Das im Jahr 1540 erbaute Castle Stalker ist ein vierstöckiges Turmhaus und eine der besterhaltenen mittelalterlichen Burgen im Westen Schottlands.

Construido en 1540, el Castillo de Stalker es una casa-torre de cuatro plantas y uno de los castillos medievales mejor conservados de Escocia oriental.

Construit en 1540, le château de Stalker, maison-tour de quatre étages, est l'un des châteaux médiévaux les mieux préservés de l'ouest de l'Écosse.

Tarbert

ARGYLL AND BUTE

The attractive village of Tarbert is situated on a narrow strip of land where West Loch Kintyre and East Loch Tarbert almost meet.

Das reizende Dorf Tarbert liegt an einer kleinen Bucht auf einer schmalen Landzunge, an der sich West Loch Kintyre und East Loch Tarbert fast treffen.

El atractivo pueblo de Tarbert está situado en una estrecha franja de tierra que separa West Loch Kintyre de East Loch Tarbert.

Le village attrayant de Tarbert est situé sur une bande de terre étroite séparant West Loch Kintyre de East Loch Tarbert.

Mount Stuart

ISLE OF BUTE, ARGYLL AND BUTE

The magnificent Victorian Gothic Mount Stuart that exists today replaced an older structure that was destroyed by fire in 1877.

Das prächtige viktorianisch-gotische Anwesen Mount Stuart, so wie es heute existiert, ersetzt ein älteres Gebäude, das 1877 durch einen Brand zerstört worden war.

La magnífica casa gótico-victoriana Mount Stuart que existe hoy en día se construyó sobre una antigua edificación que se destruyó en un incendio en 1877.

Mount Stuart, une magnifique demeure victorienne gothique, remplace un édifice plus ancien qui fut détruit par un incendie en 1877.

Kilchurn Castle

LOCH AWE, ARGYLL AND BUTE

Kilchurn Castle (previous pages), now managed by Historic Scotland, began as a five-storey tower house in 1450.

Kilchurn Castle (vorherige Seiten), das heute von Historic Scotland verwaltet wird, wurde um 1450 als fünfstöckiger Wohnturm erbaut.

El Castillo Kilchurn (doble página anterior), ahora gestionado por Historic Scotland ('Escocia Histórica'), tuvo sus comienzos en 1450 como una casa-torre de cinco plantas .

Le château Kilchurn (pages précédentes), désormais géré par l'Historic Scotland (agence écossaise des monuments historiques), était une maison-tour de cinq étages à son origine en 1450.

Dunoon

ARGYLL AND BUTE

Dunoon has long been a popular holiday destination for Glaswegians, giving rise to the phrase 'Dunoon, Dunoon is a bonnie wee toon'.

Dunoon ist ein beliebtes Ferienziel für Glasgower, wovon die Redensart „Dunoon, Dunoon ist eine hübsche kleine Stadt (*toon*)" zeugt.

Desde hace mucho tiempo que Dunoon ha sido un destino vacacional muy popular entre los habitantes de Glasgow, dando lugar a la frase 'Dunoon, Dunoon is a *bonnie wee* toon' ('Dunoon, Dunoon es una pequeña ciudad bonita').

Dunoon a longtemps été une destination populaire de vacances pour les habitants de Glasgow, donnant naissance à l'expression "Dunoon, Dunoon is a bonnie wee toon" (Dunoon, Dunooon est une jolie petite ville).

Glen Orchy

ARGYLL AND BUTE

Stretching for 19 km (12 miles), Glen Orchy is a stunning valley in which the River Orchy links Bridge of Orchy and Dalmally.

Durch das 19 km lange und überwältigend schöne Tal Glen Orchy fließt der Fluss Orchy, der die Ortschaften Bridge of Orchy und Dalmally verbindet.

Por el maravilloso valle Glen Orchy de 19 km, discurre el río Orchy que enlaza Bridge of Orchy con Dalmally

Glen Orchy est une vallée magnifique, qui s'étend sur 19 km (12 miles), dans laquelle la rivière Orchy relie Bridge of Orchy et Dalmally.

Inveraray Castle

ARGYLL AND BUTE

A mix of Baroque, Palladian and Gothic styles, Inveraray Castle was completed in 1789 and was the first of its kind in Scotland.

Das Inveraray Castle, eine Mischung aus Barock, palladianischem und gotischem Stil, wurde im Jahre 1789 fertiggestellt und war in Schottland das erste seiner Art.

Una mezcla de los estilos Barroco, Palladiano y Gótico, El Castillo Inveraray fue completado en 1789 y fue el primero de su tipo en Escocia.

Le château Inveraray, achevé en 1789, combine des styles architecturaux qui vont du gothique au baroque en passant par le palladianisme. Il fut le premier de son genre en Écosse.

Duart Castle

ISLE OF MULL, ARGYLL AND BUTE

Duart Castle has been the home of the Clan Maclean since the late fourteenth century, although parts of the building are open to the public.

Duart Castle ist seit dem späten 14. Jahrhundert der Sitz des Maclean-Clans; Teile des Gebäudes sind heute der Öffentlichkeit zugänglich.

El Castillo Duart ha sido el hogar del Clan Maclean desde los finales del siglo XIV, aunque algunas partes del edificio están abiertas al público.

Le château Duart, siège du clan MacLean depuis la fin du XIVème siècle, est en partie ouvert au public.

Rothesay

ISLE OF BUTE, ARGYLE AND BUTE

Rothesay is the main town on the Isle of Bute, and has not only an attractive harbour but also the stunning medieval Rothesay Castle.

Rothesay, die bedeutendste Stadt der Insel Bute, hat nicht nur einen reizenden Hafen, sondern beherbergt auch die beeindruckende mittelalterliche Schlossruine Rothesay Castle.

Rothesay, principal pueblo de la Isla de Bute, no sólo cuenta con un puerto atractivo, sino que también tiene el impresionante castillo medieval de Rothesay.

Rothesay, principale ville de l'île de Bute, est un port attrayant et est aussi le site d'un étonnant château médiéval.

SOUTHWEST SCOTLAND AND THE BORDERS

Heading south along the west coast is 'Burns Country'; here you will find the Brig O'Doon, featured in Burns' poem 'Tam O'Shanter', and the stunning Culzean Castle and Country Park, among other attractions.

Der Westküste entlang Richtung Süden ist „Burns Country". Hier finden Sie die Brig O'Doon, die Brücke aus Robert Burns' Gedicht „Tam O'Shanter", und neben anderen Sehenswürdigkeiten das wunderschöne Culzean Castle.

Hacía el sur y a lo largo de la costa oeste está 'Burns Country', donde se encuentra el puente Brig O Doon mencionado en el poema de Burns, 'Tam O Shanter', además del impresionante Castillo Culzean y, entre otros lugares, Country Park .

À "Burns Country" (le pays de Burns) au sud le long de la côte ouest, vous trouverez Brig 'O'Doon , représenté dans le poème de Burns' "Tam O'Shanter", ainsi que l'éblouissant château de Culzean et son parc naturel, parmi bien d'autres lieux d'intérét.

Isle of Whithorn Harbour

DUMFRIES AND GALLOWAY

The harbour has always been the Isle of Whithorn's focal point; today the fishermen make a living selling local crabs and lobsters.

Der Hafen ist seit jeher der Mittelpunkt der Insel Whithorn. Heute verdienen die Fischer ihren Lebensunterhalt durch den Verkauf von Krebsen und Hummern.

El puerto siempre ha sido el punto de encuentro de la isla de Whithorn. Hoy en día los pescadores se ganan la vida vendiendo cangrejos y langostas locales.

Le port a toujours été le centre de l'île de Whithorn; de nos jours, les pêcheurs vivent de la vente de crabes et de homards.

Mull of Galloway

DUMFRIES AND GALLOWAY

The Mull of Galloway, with its dramatic cliffs rising to 76 m (250 ft) above sea level, is Scotland's most southerly point.

Der Mull of Galloway ist mit seinen schroffen Klippen, die sich bis zu 76 Meter über den Meeresspiegel erheben, Schottlands südlichster Punkt.

Mull of Gallaway, con sus dramáticos acantilados que se elevan hasta 76 metros por encima del nivel del mar, es el punto más al sur de Escocia.

Le promontoire de Galloway, avec ses falaises qui s'élèvent à 76 m (250 pieds) d'altitude au-dessus de la mer, est le point le plus au sud de l'Écosse.

Sweetheart Abbey

NEAR DUMFRIES, DUMFRIES AND GALLOWAY

Sweetheart Abbey was so-named by the monks there, in memory of founder Lady Devorgilla of Galloway and her beloved husband.

Sweetheart Abbey wurde in Gedenken an die Gründerin Lady Devorgilla of Galloway und ihren geliebten Ehemann von den Mönchen Sweetheart („Liebling") benannt.

Sweetheart Abbey ('Abadía Cariño') fue apodada así por los monjes de la época en memoria de la fundadora, Lady Devorgilla de Galloway, y su 'querido' marido.

L'abbaye Sweetheart fut ainsi nommée par les moines, en mémoire de sa fondatrice, Lady Devorgilla de Galloway et de son mari bien-aimé.

Portpatrick

NEAR STRANRAER DUMFRIES AND GALLOWAY

A traditional harbour town, Portpatrick looks over the Irish Channel to Donaghdee. The harbour wall offers striking views of the village.

Die traditionelle Hafenstadt Portpatrick überblickt den Irischen Kanal in Richtung Donaghdee. Die Hafenmauer bietet einen beeindruckenden Blick auf den Ort.

El pueblo portuario tradicional de Portpatrick tiene vistas al Irish Channel ('Canal Irlandés') y hacía Donaghdee. Las muros del puerto ofrecen unas vistas impresionantes del pueblo.

Portpatrick est un village de pêche traditionnel qui surplombe l'Irish Channel ("la mer d'Irlande") et fait face à Donaghdee. Les remparts du port offrent une vue exceptionnelle du village.

Drumlanrig Castle

DUMFRIES AND GALLOWAY

Completed in 1691 and surrounded by the 48,600-hectare (120,000-acre) Queensberry Estate, Drumlanrig Castle has an unquestionable grandeur.

Das im Jahr 1691 fertiggestellte und vom 48,6 Hektar großen Queensberry Estate umgebene Drumlanrig Castle ist von unbestreitbarer Pracht.

Terminado en el año 1691 y rodeado por las 48.600 hectáreas de Queensberry Estate, El Castillo Drumlanrig es de una grandeza indiscutible.

Achevé en 1691 et entouré des 48.600 hectares (120.000 acres) du domaine de Queensberry, Drumlanrig Castle possède une grandeur incontestable.

Ailsa Craig

NEAR GIRVAN. AYRSHIRE

The small island of Ailsa Craig is located halfway between Glasgow and Belfast, and is affectionately known as 'Paddy's Milestone'.

Die kleine Insel Ailsa Craig liegt auf halbem Weg zwischen Glasgow und Belfast und wird liebevoll „Paddy's Milestone" genannt.

La pequeña isla Ailsa Craig se encuentra a medio camino entre Glasgow y Belfast y es conocida cariñosamente como 'Paddy s Milestone' ('El Mojón de Paddy').

La petite île d'Ailsa Craig, de par sa situation à mi-chemin entre Glasgow et Belfast, est affectueusement appelée "Paddy's Milestone" (la borne de Paddy).

Brig O'Doon

ALLOWAY, AYRSHIRE

The late-medieval Brig O'Doon is described by Robert Burns
(1759–96) in the climax of his celebrated poem 'Tam O'Shanter'.

Die spätmittelalterliche Brücke Brig O'Doon wird von Robert
Burns (1759–1796) auf dem Höhepunkt seines berühmten Gedichtes
„Tam O Shanter".beschrieben.

El puente Brig O'Doon de la Baja Edad Medieval es descrito por
Robert Burns (1759–96) en el clímax de su poema célebre
'Tam O Shanter'.

Brig O'Doon, datant de la fin du Moyen Age, est décrit
par Robert Burns (1759–96) à l'apogée de son célèbre poème
"Tam O'Shanter".

Culzean Castle

AYRSHIRE

Perched above the Firth of Clyde, with views across to the Isle of Arran, Culzean is one of the finest Georgian castles in the country.

Das über dem Firth of Clyde gelegene Culzean Castle ist mit seinem Blick auf die Insel Arran eines der schönsten Georganischen Schlösser im Land.

Encaramado sobre el Firth of Clyde ('Fiordo de Forth') y con vistas hacía la Isla de Arran, Culzean es uno de los mejores castillos georgianos de todo el país.

Culzean, l'un des plus beaux châteaux de style géorgien du pays, surplombe le Firth of Clyde, et offre une vue sur l'île d'Arran.

Goatfell

ISLE OF ARRAN

One of the many beautiful sights to be found.on the Isle of Arran, the magnificent Goatfell rises to 880 m (2886 ft) at its summit.

Als eine der vielen schönen Sehenswürdigkeiten der Insel Arran erhebt sich der eindrucksvolle Berg Goatfell auf eine Gipfelhöhe von 880 Metern.

Uno de los muchos lugares hermosos que se encuentran en la Isla de Arran, el magnífico Goatfell se eleva a 880 metros de altura.

Le Goatfell, qui s'élève à 880 mètres (2886 pieds) d'altitude, est un des plus beaux sites de l'île d'Arran.

Thirlestane Castle

LAUDER, BORDERS

The splendid red sandstone Thirlestane Castle combines the Scottish baronial style with touches of the Renaissance.

Das aus rotem Sandstein gebaute prächtige Thirlestane Castle vereint den schottischen Baronial Style mit Einflüssen der Renaissance.

El espléndido Castillo Thirlestane, hecho de arenisca roja, combina el estilo señorial escocés con toques del Renacimiento.

Le splendide château de Thirlestane en grès rouge allie le style seigneurial écossais aux influences de la Renaissance.

Manderston House

NEAR DUNS, BORDERS

Built in the 1790s and recreated between 1890 and 1905, Manderston House is one of Scotland's finest Edwardian country houses.

Das Manderston House, das ursprünglich um 1790 erbaut und zwischen 1890 und 1905 neu errichtet wurde, ist eines der schönsten Edwardischen Landhäuser Schottlands.

Construida en los años 1790 y renovada entre 1890 y 1905, Manderston House es una de las casas señoriales eduardianas más bellas de Escocia.

Construite dans les années 1790 et rénovée entre 1890 et 1905, Manderston House est l'une des plus belles demeures de l'époque Édouardienne d'Écosse.

St Abb's Head

BORDERS

With 78 hectares (192 acres) of coastline, St Abb's Head is a National Nature Reserve and hosts one of the most important seabird colonies in the UK.

St Abb's Head ist ein 78 Hektar großes Küstennaturschutzgebiet und beherbergt eine der wichtigsten Meeresvögelkolonien im Vereinigten Königreich.

Con 78 hectáreas de costa, St Abb's Head es una Reserva Natural Nacional que alberga una de las colonias de aves marinas más importantes del Reino Unido.

Réserve naturelle nationale avec 78 hectares (192 acres) de côtes, Head St Abb, abrite l'une des plus importantes colonies d'oiseaux marins du Royaume-Uni.

Jedburgh Abbey

BORDERS

Jedburgh Abbey was founded in 1138, although fragments of Celtic stonework remain that date back to the ninth century.

Jedburgh Abbey wurde im Jahr 1138 gegründet, es sind jedoch noch Fragmente eines keltischen Mauernwerks vorhanden, die aus dem 9. Jahrhundert stammen.

La Abadía de Jedburgh fue fundada en el año 1138 aunque conserva fragmentos de mampostería celta que datan del siglo IX.

L'abbaye de Jedburgh fut fondée en 1138, même si on peut encore voir dans la maçonnerie des vestiges celtiques datant du IXème siècle.

Traquair House

NEAR PEEBLES, BORDERS

Now a popular business and wedding venue, Traquair House dates back to 1107 and has entertained many royal guests over the centuries.

■■■ Traquair House, das heute für Unternehmensveranstaltungen und Hochzeiten beliebt ist, geht auf 1107 zurück und hat im Laufe der Jahrhunderte viele königlichen Gäste unterhalten.

■■■ La ahora popular empresa y lugar de celebraciones de bodas, Traquair House se remonta al año 1107 y ha albergado a numerosos invitados reales a través de los siglos.

■■■ Maintenant un commerce florissant et un lieu de mariage, Traquair House date de 1107 et fut le lieu de divertissement de nombreux invités royaux au cours des siècles.

Melrose Abbey

BORDERS

The original Melrose Abbey burned to the ground in 1385, but this ornate fifteenth-century place of worship rose in its place.

Die ursprüngliche Melrose Abbey brannte 1385 bis auf die Grundmauern ab, an ihrer Stelle entstand im 15. Jahrhundert dieses kunstvolle Gotteshaus.

La Abadía Melrose original fue reducida a cenizas en 1385, pero este lugar de adoración ornamental del siglo XV se erigió en el lugar.

La batisse d'origine de l'abbaye de Melrose fut détruite par les flammes en 1385, et à sa place fut érigé ce lieu de culte très orné datant du XVème siècle.

Abbotsford

NEAR GALASHIELS, BORDERS

Abbotsford, situated on the banks of the River Tweed, was the home of
the nineteenth-century novelist Sir Walter Scott.

Abbotsford liegt an den Ufern des Flusses Tweed und war im 19.
Jahrhundert der Wohnsitz des Schriftstellers Sir Walter Scott.

Abbotsford, situado junto al río Tweed, fue el hogar del novelista
del siglo XIX Sir Walter Scott.

Abbotsford, situé sur les bords de la rivière Tweed, fut la maison
de Sir Walter Scott, écrivain du XIXème siècle.

Glossary ❋ Glossar ❋ Glosario ❋ Glossaire

Baronial style An architectural style that formed part of the Gothic revival and was popular from the early nineteenth to the early twentieth centuries.

Ein rchitektonischer Stil, der Teil der historistischen Neugotik war und der vom frühen 19. bis zum frühen 20. Jahrhundert beliebt war.

Un estilo de arquitectura que formó parte del renacimiento gótico y fue popular desde principios del siglo XIX hasta principios del siglo XX.

Un style architectural qui a fait partie de la renaissance gothique et a été populaire du début du XIXème siècle au début du XXème siècle.

Bonnie Pretty, beautiful.

Hübsch, schön.

Bonito, hermoso.

Joli(e), beau ou belle

Clan A group of families sharing a common surname, ancestor and leader.

Eine Gruppe von Familien, die den gleichen Nachnamen, Vorfahren oder Anführer haben.

Un grupo de familias que comparten un mismo apellido, antepasados y líder.

Un groupe de familles qui partagent le même nom et ancêtres et sont sous la conduite d'un chef.

Gaelic The Scottish Gaelic language has been spoken in Scotland since before Roman times, although it is now in severe decline.

(Gaelisch) Wurde in Schottland schon vor der Römerzeit gesprochen, seine Verbreitung geht jetzt aber deutlich zurück.

El idioma gaélico escocés se habla en Escocia desde antes de la época romana, aunque ahora se halla en grave declive.

Le language gaélique écossais a été parlé en Écosse bien avant l'époque romaine, mais il est maintenant en sérieux déclin.

Glen A narrow, secluded valley.

Ein schmales, abseits gelegenes Tal.

Un valle estrecho y apartado

Une vallée étroite et isolée.

Wee Small, tiny.

Klein, winzig.

Pequeño, diminuto.

Petit, minuscule.

Haggis A Scottish dish made with offal, oatmeal, onions and suet, boiled in a sheep's stomach.

Un plato escocés hecho con menudos, copos de avena, cebolla y sebo, hervido en el estómago de una oveja.

Un plato Escocés hecho con achuras, copos de avena, cebolla y sebo, hervido en el estómago de una oveja.

Un plat écossais préparé avec des abats, de la farine d'avoine, des oignons et de la graisse, et bouilli dans l'estomac d'un mouton.

Laird The owner of an estate, similar to the English 'Lord'.

Schottischer Gutsbesitzer, ähnlich dem englischen „Lord".

El dueño de una propiedad, similar a un 'Lord' inglés. Terrateniente.

Le propriétaire d'un domaine, comparable au titre de ''Lord'' en Angleterre.

Loch A lake.

Ein See.

Un lago.

Un lac.

Military Tattoo Annual music and dance display involving the armed forces and a range of other performers.

Jährliches Musik- und Tanzfest, an dem die Streitkräfte und eine Reihe von anderen Künstlern teilnehmen.

Espectáculo anual de música y danza que involucra a las fuerzas armadas y a una variedad de otros intérpretes.

Défilé militaire annuel de musique et danse exécuté par des fanfares militaires et une grande variété d'exécutants.

Sea loch An arm of the sea or a long, narrow bay.

Un brazo del mar o una bahía larga y estrecha.

Un brazo del mar o una bahía larga y estrecha.

Un bras de mer ou une longue baie étroite.

INDEX